CY YOUNG WINNERS

Marty Nabhan

The Rourke Corporation, Inc.
Vero Beach, Florida 32964

The Rourke Corporation, Inc.
P.O. Box 3328, Vero Beach, FL 32964

Nabhan, Marty.
    Cy Young winners / by Marty Nabhan.
        p. cm .— (Baseball heroes)
    Includes bibliographical references (p. 46) and index.
    Summary: Highlights great pitching moments and great pitchers in the history of baseball, with an emphasis on those players who have won the Cy Young Award.
    ISBN 0-86593-133-X
    1. Pitchers (Baseball)—United States—Biography—Juvenile literature. 2. Cy Young Award—Juvenile literature. [1. Cy Young Award. 2. Baseball players. 3. Baseball—History.]
  I. Title. II. Series.
GV865.A1N33   1991
796.357'092—dc20   91-11371
[B]   CIP
                                                                              AC

Series Editor: Gregory Lee
Editor: Marguerite Aronowitz
Book design and production: The Creative Spark, Capistrano Beach, CA
Cover photograph: Marc S. Levine/New York Mets
Consultant: Rick Albrecht

Contents

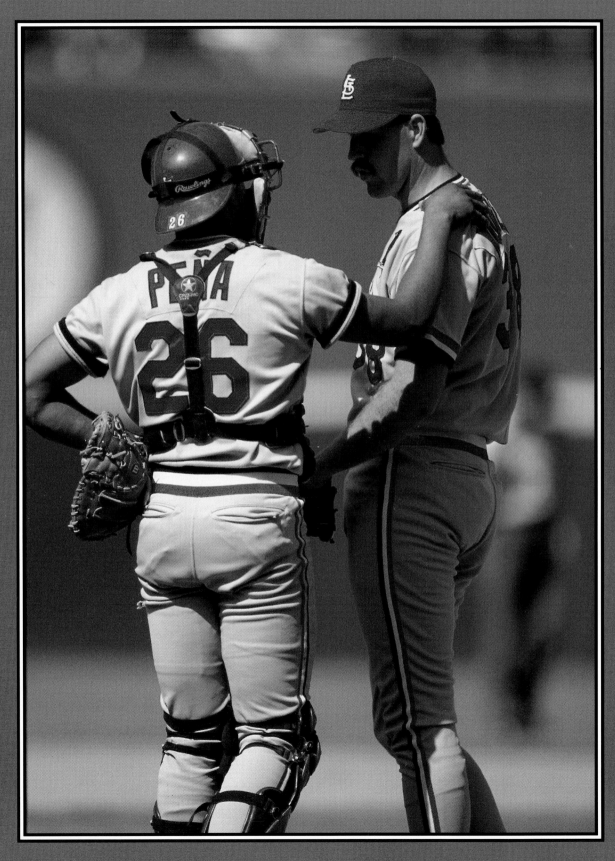

The pitcher, with the help of his catcher, controls the pace of a baseball game.

The Pitcher

Baseball is a game between two teams of nine players. At least, that is what the official rules of the game say. Actually, the nine players on each team never face each other directly at the same time. It's not like football, where 11 players on offense try to move the ball against 11 players on defense. Nor is it like basketball, which pits five players from each team running up and down the court against each other. Nor is it like soccer, hockey, or any other major team sport in America.

During a baseball game, much of the action takes place between two players: the pitcher and the hitter. It is the pitcher who controls the game. He decides when to pitch. He decides how to pitch. Then he pitches.

Some people have said pitching is 70 percent of baseball. Others have said it's 80 percent. Whatever the number, we might say the pitcher is the most important player on the field.

The Cy Young Award is baseball's highest honor for pitchers.

A Storybook Season

Scene: Game 5 of the 1988 World Series, Oakland Coliseum.

Teams: The powerful Oakland Athletics vs. the underdog Los Angeles Dodgers.

Background: The Oakland A's are on a roll. Their record of 104 wins in the regular season is third best in the American League over the past 30 years. One of the great teams in baseball, they march into the Series

The record for most scoreless innings in a row belongs to Orel Hershiser (59), hurling the Dodgers into the World Series in 1988.

ready to be crowned as champs. The Dodgers have a team that one television announcer calls "perhaps the weakest in World Series history." But surprisingly, going into Game 5, the Dodgers hold the Series lead 3 games to 1. In the ninth inning of Game 5, they're ahead 5-2. *Action:* Orel Hershiser walks out to the pitcher's mound to finish one of the greatest seasons a pitcher ever had. There's no doubt in his mind, he can do it. He does.

"Does everyone really appreciate what Orel has done?" asked then-Dodger star Kirk Gibson. "I don't know if we will ever again see the likes of what he's done...It may be that no pitcher in history stayed in that kind of groove so long or so well."

What was "that kind of groove"? To put it simply, it was a good, solid year with a storybook ending. Hershiser's record was 23 wins and 8 losses. But the way he finished the season was absolutely incredible.

First, he broke a Major League record by not giving up a run for 59 innings in a row. Don Drysdale, who held the record of 58-2/3 scoreless innings since 1968, was the first person out of the dugout to congratulate Hershiser.

Then it was time for Hershiser and the Dodgers to face the New York Mets for the National League playoffs. Most people thought the Mets would win easily. They led the league in hitting, pitching, victories, and many other categories. But Hershiser was just getting warmed up. He appeared in four of the seven games, three times as a starter and once as a reliever. He gave up only three runs total, and in Game 7, pitched a shutout that gave the Dodgers the National League title. Oakland and the World Series were next. In Game 2, Orel showed that he wasn't only a great pitcher. He tied a World Series batting record by batting 1.000, getting hits all three times at bat. That equaled the total number of hits he gave up in Game 2 to the entire Oakland team.

In Game 5, as Hershiser took the mound, only three outs stood between him and the storybook season's happy ending. Oakland power hitter Mark McGuire was the first to fall. Next, catcher Ron Hassey struck out. Oakland third baseman Carney Lansford added to the drama by getting a single, then stealing second and third while Hershiser pitched to Tony Phillips. But Phillips swung on the third strike and the game was over. Hershiser took a few steps off the mound and looked skyward before being mobbed by his teammates. It was the perfect ending to a great year, a remarkable year—a Cy Young year.

Cy Young: the award that bears his name celebrates the best pitchers in baseball.

Cy Young

Y is for Young
The magnificent Cy;
People batted against him,
But I never knew why.
—*Ogden Nash*

A whistle was heard in a small farm town in Ohio in 1890. But it wasn't the whistle of a farmer working in his field. It was the sizzling whistle of a pitcher's fastball. A baseball scout came to see this pitcher for himself, and liked what he saw. With an offer of $40 a month, the scout lured the youth to Canton to play pro ball. The young man was named Denton True Young.

Young possessed an incredible fastball— perhaps the fastest ever seen. With no formal training, Young relied on his sheer speed to overpower hitters. A sportswriter compared Young to a cyclone, and the nickname "Cy" stuck.

Cy won 15 games for Canton that year, and lost 15. But

Pitcher Trivia

Q: Who was the youngest Cy Young winner of all time?
A: Dwight Gooden, New York Mets, 20 years old—15 days younger than Valenzuela when he won.

Q: Who was the first relief pitcher to win the Cy Young?
A: Mike Marshall, Los Angeles Dodgers, 1974.

Q: Who was the oldest Cy Young winner?
A: Early Wynn, Chicago White Sox, 39 years old, 1959.

even though his record was average, his raw talent drew interest from major league teams, and Canton offered Cy's contract to the majors for $500. Cap Anson of the Chicago White Stockings saw Cy and dismissed him as "just a big ol' farmer." That opinion would soon change.

Davis Hawley, an official for the Cleveland Spiders, bought Cy's contract and put him to work immediately against Cap Anson and Chicago. Cy Young allowed only one run in three hits against Chicago in an 8-1 victory. More importantly, he struck Anson out twice.

"The big rube had a lot of luck beating us," Anson said to Hawley afterward. "He's too inexperienced to help you much. But I'm willing to give you $1,000 for him. I think I could help him to get better."

Hawley replied, "Keep your $1,000. We'll keep the rube."

That was just the start. Cy Young went on to set about every record in baseball. In a career that lasted 22 years, he had 20 or more victories in 16 seasons. He had 30 wins in five of those seasons. He pitched a perfect game (no hits, no walks) in 1904, and was one walk away on two other occasions (in 1897 and 1908). All told, Cy pitched three no-hitters in his career, the final one when he was 41 years old!

Adding to his vicious fastball, Cy practiced his curveball, and gained even greater control. Every time people thought Cy had lost his ability, he simply developed a new pitch or was picked up by a team that believed in him. After starting with Canton, he played with Cleveland, St. Louis, and the Boston Red Sox (of the newly formed American League), went back to Cleveland, and finished up with the Boston Braves.

"I believe in putting the ball over the plate for hitting, trusting to the fielders, in this way saving your arm," Cy said. "A pitcher amounts to but very little unless his pitching arm is strong." This explains Cy's ability to play so well for so many years.

In 1911 Cy retired, having won more than 200 games in both the American and National Leagues. In all, he totaled 511 wins, a record that still stands today.

The Award

The year was 1956, one year after the death of Cy Young, and Fred Frick was concerned. Frick, the former commissioner of baseball, noticed that very few pitchers were being selected as Most Valuable Players (MVPs). The award usually went to players who played every day. Pitchers needed time to rest their arms between games. They only pitched every fourth or fifth day, no matter how good they were. Frick knew the impact pitchers had on the game, and wanted a way to honor them as well.

Frick came up with the idea for the Cy Young Award, an award especially for pitchers. He gave the responsibility of voting to the Baseball Writers Association of America (BBWAA). It would be their task to choose the best pitcher each year.

The award began in 1956 and was given out once a year until 1966. Since 1967 the award has been given to two pitchers each year. William Eckert, the new baseball commissioner, decided that the American and National Leagues should each have their own Cy Young winner.

The Silent Winner

Scene: Game 6 of the 1980 World Series.
Teams: The Philadelphia Phillies vs. the Kansas City Royals.
Background: Two-time Cy Young winner Steve Carlton has had a strange career. Often he follows a winning season with a losing one. Early in his career, the press said he lacked concentration. Since then, he's refused to speak with them. No interviews, no statements, no

Ace Dave Stieb hurled the first no-hitter in Blue Jays' history.

nothing. He simply dedicated himself to his game, and became silent to all but his close friends. Now at age 35, and with his team up 4 games to 1, he has a chance to silence his critics once and for all.

Action: Steve Carlton focuses in on the batter. When he takes the mound, everything else is unimportant. The crowd becomes a blur. He knows his teammates can take care of themselves. Carlton's own 24-9 record and 2.34 ERA didn't matter either. It's just one batter at a time, taking all of Steve's concentration. Carlton's slider zips over the plate. Through seven innings, he holds the Royals scoreless. But in the eighth he tires, and a relief pitcher is brought in to finish. Steve Carlton leaves to a standing ovation.

Carlton had every reason to be tired. He worked harder on and off season than anyone in baseball. His workouts even included weight lifting, almost unheard of for a pitcher. And Carlton put that power in every pitch.

As Carlton watched the rest of Game 6, his teammates hung on to win, 4-1. In the locker room, members of the press searched to find Carlton. Did he think he would win his third Cy Young? (He would, and a fourth later.) How did it feel to finally win a Series? How did he develop the control he lacked early in his career?

Alas, they never found out. While the rest of the team whooped it up, Steve sat alone in the training room, quietly sipping his champagne. The silent champion would stay silent.

Mark Davis had a Cy Young-winning season in 1989 with a 1.85 ERA, followed by a terrible 1990 with a 2-7 record.

Early Greats

Baseball in the 1800s was still changing. Today we take the rules for granted. But in the beginning, the rules developed slowly over a period of time. For example, the distance from the pitcher's mound to home, the number of strikes and balls, whether there should be strikes and balls—all these changed to perfect the game. And they changed with the development of the role of the pitcher. You might say the history of pitching was the history of baseball.

The Cy Young Award has only been given for the last 34 years. That leaves more than one hundred years of baseball without a so-called "best pitcher." So here are a few of the early greats who helped make the game of baseball what it is today.

In 1858 a young pitcher was getting attention. Seventeen-year-old Jim Creighton was adding a snap to his wrist when he pitched the ball. At that time, all pitching was done underhanded. His pitches were faster than any others. This "fastball" not only made Creighton famous; he became the first baseball player to get paid, and that's when baseball went professional.

Although no one is quite sure who threw the first "curveball," the credit is often given to William Arthur "Candy" Cummings. One day he was throwing clam shells at the beach with friends. He noticed how the shells curved through the air. Being a pitcher, Cummings imagined what it would be like if he could get a baseball to do the same thing. He practiced and practiced, never quite getting it right. Then, during a game, he noticed a lot of batters swinging at his pitches and missing. Indeed—as he watched the ball leave his hand—it curved before reaching the plate. He had "invented" the curveball.

Dave Stewart had yet to win the Cy Young by 1990 despite four straight 20-game seasons.

Bobby Mathews made history in 1868 by spitting on a baseball and throwing it. His "spitter" caused the ball to dip, curve, drop, and do a number of other things. The spitter was legal until 1920—but nobody wanted to catch it!

The turn of the century and the early 1900s brought a new style of pitcher. The game of baseball was settling down to our modern rules. A pitcher now had to have more than just one good pitch. This was the era of Cy Young and many other pitchers who achieved fame during this period.

Christy Mathewson and Grover Cleveland Alexander are tied for third place on the all-time win list with 361 victories apiece.

In 1911 Alexander won 28 games as a rookie, a record that still stands. Alexander is noteworthy because he pitched so well in his later years. When he was 39, he came into Game 7 of the 1926 World Series with bases loaded in the seventh inning, and pitched the St. Louis Cardinals to a victory over the Yankees.

Mathewson's strength was his variety. "He was the perfect pitcher," said his catcher Roger Bresnahan. "He always pitched to the batter's weakness. He had all kinds of stuff and he knew just where to use it." And more often than not, his "stuff" earned him a victory.

But many consider Walter Johnson to be the greatest pitcher of all time. Second to Young in all-time victories with 416, Johnson possessed a lightning-fast pitch. Batters complained, "You can't hit what you can't see." He is first in career shutouts (110), and holds a lifetime ERA of 2.17.

Carl Hubbell threw a pitch that would break in toward a right-handed hitter. If thrown by a left-hander, it breaks away from a right-handed hitter (or in toward a left-handed hitter). Hubbell named it the screwball. In an all-star game, he used it to strike out five future hall-

The only National League pitcher to ever win the Cy Young three times in a row was the Dodgers' Sandy Koufax.

of-famers in a row, including Babe Ruth and Lou Gehrig. Carl also won the Most Valuable Player award twice—hard to do for a pitcher.

We may never know how great Satchel Paige really was. Because of the color barrier in baseball, Paige spent most of his years in the Negro leagues. He had great control, and was extremely accurate. People thought he was too old to pitch when he was finally given the chance in the Major Leagues in 1948. But the 42-year-old Paige proved them wrong. Joe DiMaggio called him "the best and the fastest pitcher I've ever

18

faced." Unbelievably, Paige pitched a game for the Kansas City A's when he was 59.

Perfection

Scene: September 5, 1965, in the heat of a pennant race, Los Angeles.

Teams: Chicago Cubs vs. the Los Angeles Dodgers.

Background: Sandy Koufax almost didn't play this year as his pitching elbow is plagued with painful arthritis. The elbow swells up after each game. Koufax has to soak his arm in ice to be ready for his next start. So far this year, Koufax hasn't missed a start. By September 5, the Dodgers are in a heated race for first place.

Action: Koufax's arm is feeling okay tonight, but not great. He starts out slowly. Although he retires the first nine batters, his timing is slightly off. His fastball is a bit wild. Midway through the game, Koufax finds the groove. His fastball is back. His curve is perfect. Batters are swinging at the air. It's the seventh inning. With two out, Koufax faces Billy Williams and quickly gets behind, 3 balls and no strikes. Koufax winds up and throws. Strike one. Another pitch, another strike. With the count 3-2, Williams pops up and the inning is over. Koufax faces six more batters, and strikes out all six.

The game ended with the Dodgers on top, 1-0. Sandy Koufax had faced 27 batters and fanned 14. More importantly, he gave up no hits and no walks, posting one of the few perfect games in history. It was his fourth no-hitter. He went on to win his second of three Cy Young Awards that year. Unfortunately, arthritis in his pitching arm forced him to quit after the following season, at the height of his career.

But for one night, Sandy Koufax was perfect.

Award-winner Frank Viola (1988) became the 18th pitcher to have 20-win seasons in both leagues.

The Golden Age

The dominant team of the '50s and early '60s was the New York Yankees. During a 15-year period, they were in the World Series 11 times. Pitcher "Whitey" Ford was one of the reasons. Behind a deceptive fastball, Ford won 236 games in his career and won the Cy Young Award in 1961. He also started in 22 World Series games.

In his career, Warren Spahn won 20 games or more 13 times, second only to Cy Young. Spahn was consistent. His manager called him "my go-to-sleep pitcher. I can go to bed the night before Spahn pitches and get a good night's sleep." Spahn is fifth in all-time wins with 363, but first for left-handed pitchers.

From 1962 to 1966, Los Angeles cornered the market in Cy Young Awards. The Dodgers' Don Drysdale won in 1962, and Sandy Koufax took the honors in 1963, '65, and '66. In 1964 the Los Angeles Angels had newcomer Dean Chance to give the crowd a thrill. Chance had a 1.56 ERA in 1964, the lowest in the majors, and took home the Cy Young.

With Drysdale and Koufax, the Dodgers had the best one-two punch in baseball. Drysdale was the good, solid performer. The Dodgers counted on him to pitch well: they didn't give him many runs to work with. His losses were often 1-0, 2-1, or 2-0. In 1962, Koufax went out with an injury. It was up to Drysdale to carry the team. Drysdale had his best year, going 25-9 and earning Cy Young honors.

The Year of the Pitcher

The year 1968 is sometimes called the "year of the

St. Louis hurler Bob Gibson was also named MVP when he won the Cy Young in 1968 with an ERA of 1.12 and 22 wins.

pitcher." In the '60s, pitchers brought back the knuckler and forkball. The knuckler is thrown with either the knuckles or fingertips, which reduces the spin on the ball. Unfortunately, the ball reacts differently every time. The forkball is also called the split-finger fastball. The ball is stuck between the index and middle finger. Thrown like a fastball, it flies slower and drops at the last second.

In 1968 Drysdale pitched a record six straight shutouts, and 58-2/3 innings of scoreless baseball. In spite of his great streak, however, pitching's highest honor went to Bob Gibson of the St. Louis Cardinals.

Gibson was sick a lot as a boy. He had hay fever,

asthma, pneumonia, rickets, and rheumatic heart. But this didn't stop him. He worked hard to become a good athlete, and when he was finally given a chance to start with the Cardinals, he kept getting better and better. Gibson practiced his batting, too, and became one of the best hitting pitchers in baseball.

He pitched his St. Louis Cardinals to victory over the Yankees in Game 7 of the 1964 World Series. In the 1967 World Series against the Boston Red Sox, he was amazing. First he pitched a six-hitter in Game 1 for a 2-1 victory. Then in Game 4 he pitched a five-hit shutout, 6-0. In Game 7, he faced Boston ace (and 1967 Cy Young winner) Jim Lonborg. But Gibson was unstoppable. He struck out ten batters, hit a home run, and won the game and Series, 7-2.

In 1968, Gibson pitched 13 shutouts—5 in a row. At one point in the season he challenged Drysdale's "scoreless inning" record. His ERA in '68 was an incredible 1.12. He had a record of 22-9, won the National League Cy Young, and got the chance to go against Denny McLain and the Detroit Tigers for the World Series.

The 1968 World Series was dubbed "The Battle of the Pitchers." Rowdy Denny McLain, at 24, did the unthinkable for Detroit that year: he won 31 games! In Game 1, Gibson struck out 17 hitters for a new Series record. And the records didn't stop there. Gibson finished the Series with 35 strikeouts and added a home run to his credit, giving him two in Series competition lifetime, a record for a pitcher.

But the Cardinals still lost. The Series went to McLain and the Tigers. McLain and Gibson *both* received the Cy Young Award and Most Valuable Player Award, the first time a player was ever voted them unanimously. It was a fitting climax to the year of the pitcher.

Doug Drabek—the 1990 Cy Young victor in the National League.

The Miracle Mets

Scene: Game 4 of the 1969 World Series.

Teams: The New York Mets vs. the Baltimore Orioles.

Background: The Mets stink. They're one of the worst teams in baseball history, but they're lovable losers, and have many fans. In 1969 things are finally turning around for them. With star pitcher Tom Seaver, they find themselves in the World Series, up against the Orioles and American League Cy Young Winner Mike Cuellar. The Mets don't stand a chance. Oh, yes…and it's Game 4 and the Mets are up 2 games to 1.

Action: The Mets believe. The country is starting to believe, too. But a stumbling block is in the way: the Orioles have a great starting lineup and is one of the ten best teams in history. Surely it will be a tough test, but Seaver is ready for the challenge. He pitches eight scoreless innings, but this is not enough. Going into the ninth, Seaver tries to protect the fragile 1-0 lead. With one out and runners on first and third, Oriole Brooks Robinson comes up to hit. The great third baseman hits a shot to center—it looks like a game-winner.

Ron Swoboda comes running up, diving forward to make a backhanded catch just inches above the grass. The runner on third scores, but Seaver gets out of the inning deadlocked 1-1.

The game goes into extra innings, but the Mets are not to be denied. In the bottom of the tenth, a misjudged fly ball puts a runner on second. The next batter walks, and when J. C. Martin bunts, the throw to first hits him on the wrist. The ball bounces harmlessly to second and the run scores. The "Miracle" Mets, up 3 games to 1, win. The next day they put away the Series.

Seaver finished the year with a 25-7 record and a 2.21 ERA. He won the Cy Young—an award he would win two more times.

Bruce Sutter had 37 saves in 1979, the year he won the National League Cy Young Award.

The 1970s

Baseball is a game of adjustments, both on the field and off. On the field, the pitcher keeps his eyes and ears open for any adjustment that needs to be made. His job is to keep the other team from scoring.

Pitchers have an incredible ability to adjust. They develop new pitches. They learn about the hitters. They get information from the catcher. And as each season goes by they keep getting better.

Off the field, adjustments are made as well. As the pitchers get better, baseball officials try to think of ways to help the batters. The officials' job is to keep the game exciting.

Changes have been made. The pitcher's mound was lowered from 15 inches to 10 inches. The strike zone was reduced. The designated hitter was introduced in the American League. As a result, scoring went up. In the '70s, the league was dominated by a few pitchers fortunate enough to win the Cy Young.

For the six

Pitcher's Trivia

Q: Who were the only brothers to both win the Cy Young?
A: Jim Perry, Minnesota Twins (1970); Gaylord Perry, Cleveland Indians (1972) and San Diego Padres (1978).

Q: Who was the first Cy Young winner from a team that didn't win a pennant the same year?
A: Don Drysdale, Los Angeles Dodgers, 1962.

Q: What pitcher won 25 or more games in three different seasons, and still didn't win the Cy Young Award?
A: Juan Marichal, in 1963, 1966, and 1968.

years from 1967 to 1972, Ferguson Jenkins won at least 20 games each season with the Chicago Cubs. It was the first time since Christy Mathewson that a right-handed National Leaguer had been so consistent. Although he only won the Cy Young Award once, his fastball, curve, and control made him one of the most respected pitchers in baseball. And Jenkins never played on a pennant winner, which makes his 284 career victories even more impressive.

Another consistent pitcher was Jim Palmer of the Baltimore Orioles. He won 20 games or more in eight out of nine seasons (although never six in a row). He was a perfectionist. Even though he suffered with a bad back most of his career, he believed in going nine strong innings with no bad pitches. His three Cy Youngs and career 2.86 ERA show how committed he was. His battles with manager and good friend Earl Weaver were famous. Weaver used to joke, "See these gray hairs? Every one of them has 22 (Palmer's number) on it."

Gaylord Perry brought laughs back to the game. His greaseball antics are so legendary that they filled a book. He was never overpowering, but hitters feared him anyway. The crazy moves his pitches would make made them impossible to hit. Perry won the Cy Young in both the American and National Leagues, the only pitcher to do so. He saved wear and tear on his arm by perfecting the greaseball. This let him play many years, and he ended his career with 314 wins.

In the early '70s, the Oakland A's were baseball's dominant team. The ace on their staff was young Jim "Catfish" Hunter. Hunter earned fame quickly by pitching a perfect game in 1968. He was known for his great control, and threw strikes to get hitters out instead of trying to fool them. His great accuracy made that possible. But after he was traded to the Yankees in 1975, he pitched too often and ruined his arm. He

*World Series MVP Jose Rijo (1990) held down Oakland A's
hitting with a 0.59 average.*

suffered from injuries the rest of his career, and never quite attained the success he had with Oakland.

Tom Seaver has often been called the greatest pitcher in the modern era of baseball. He had all the necessary qualities: speed, technique, control, endurance, and intelligence. His accomplishments with the lowly Mets became legendary the year they occurred. He was a strikeout king, 300-game winner (311), and had a lifetime ERA of 2.82, one of the lowest in baseball.

One Slick Customer

Scene: May 31, 1964, in New York City, the longest game in baseball history.

Teams: The San Francisco Giants vs. the New York Mets.

Background: The game is in the 13th inning. Giant manager Al Dark has no other choice: he waves Gaylord Perry into the game. Perry is an average pitcher. But in practice he's been working on a new pitch, a pitch he's perfected, a pitch that will change his career.

Action: Perry faces the batter. It's the perfect time to use his new pitch. He goes through a series of movements, hurls the ball, and it zips into the dirt. The ball flies as though it is defying the laws of nature. Certainly no normal ball could fly like that. But this is no normal ball. Perry had just thrown his first spitter.

"Use less spit," Perry's catcher warns with a laugh. "The umpire is getting suspicious of that splashing sound in my mitt."

The game goes into extra innings—23 total, to be exact. The winning pitcher is Perry.

Even though the spitter had been illegal since 1920, many pitchers continued to throw it. They practiced the art of concealment. Perry raised that art to a whole new level. He used spit, sweat, grease, petroleum jelly—anything that would make the ball perform the way he wanted it to.

And he hid it anywhere. Sometimes a thin layer of petroleum jelly on his neck would do the job. Other times, he hid it on a fingernail. Just a drop or smudge was all he needed. He even had a small tube in his pocket. Once when he slid into home, the bat boy had to dive for the forbidden gel before the umpire saw it. If the umpire ever did see it, he could eject, suspend or fine Perry.

When Perry moved to the Cleveland Indians of the American League in 1972, the fame of his spitball followed him. Manager Billy Martin once sent a bloodhound to sniff out the mound for Perry's petroleum jelly. That was the year Perry won 24 games—the first person to win more than 20 in both leagues since Cy Young. Perry followed in his brother Jim's footsteps by winning the Cy Young, and repeated the feat in 1978 with the San Diego Padres. He was the only pitcher to win the award in both leagues.

On the mound and checking the catcher's signs: Kansas City's Bret Saberhagen.

The Makings of a Winner

Just what makes a Cy Young winner? Is it a blistering fastball? A sinking slider? Is it knowing the batter's strengths and weaknesses? Here's a look at a number of things that help, and the pitchers who make them work.

To make it in the majors, great pitchers all need to have control—the ability to put the ball across the plate. One good sign of having control is the lack of walks permitted. LaMarr Hoyt with the Chicago White Sox showed great control in his 1983 Cy Young season. He won 14 in a row at the end of the season. Chicago Cub Rick Sutcliffe made control a fine art. He had the ability to hit the corners of the strike zone, a key to having control. Reliever Willie Hernandez of the Detroit Tigers came out of the bullpen to relieve with control. His 32 saves out of 33 tries in 1984 was a Cy Young Award demonstration of control.

Perhaps the king of control in recent years is Bret Saberhagen of the Kansas City Royals. Saberhagen displayed his control in winning two Cy Young Awards (1985, 1989) and leading his team to victory in the 1985 World Series.

Any complete arsenal begins with the pitches thrown. Some pitchers specialize. For example, Orel Hershiser lives off the sinking slider, and Bob Welch of the Oakland A's has a strong fastball. Dodger Fernando Valenzuela brought the screwball back, and Chicago Cub reliever Bruce Sutter had the split-finger fastball.

The screwball of Fernando Valenzuela made him the only pitcher in major league history to win both the Cy Young and Rookie of the Year awards in the same year (1981).

Mike Scott of the Houston Astros had great success with the split-finger. In 1986 he won 18 games, struck out 306, and led the Astros to the National League playoffs. There he beat the Mets twice. At the end of 1986, Scott's pitch was as tough to hit as Koufax's curve, Carlton's slider, or Nolan Ryan's fastball.

Then there are a few gifted pitchers who seem to have it all.

Roger Clemens of the Boston Red Sox had one of the fastest fastballs of the '80s. Mixed with his excellent curve, he was at times unstoppable. All this and control too. People have compared him to Tom Seaver. Clemens is also a student of the game—a serious pitcher anxious to learn. He started out the 1986 season by winning his first 14 games, striking out 20 batters in one of them.

Today, however, the pitcher that all other pitchers are compared to is Dwight "Doc" Gooden of the New York Mets. Gooden has good speed (a 90-100 mph fastball), a great curve, and a changeup. The most impressive thing is that he showed all the talent at such an early age. Gooden was the youngest Cy Young Award winner ever. Although Gooden has had his personal problems, he has a natural ability that could make him great for another 10 years.

In 1986, Gooden and the Mets squared off against Clemens and the Red Sox in what was the greatest World Series of recent memory. The seven-game classic pitted the two young stars against each other, with the Mets coming out on top.

The pitcher also has an advantage if his catcher is great. The catcher traditionally calls the pitch. Being the closest man on the team to the batter, the catcher can detect the slightest things that will help the pitcher. The catcher knows the opposing team as well as his own pitcher's strengths and weaknesses. "Sometimes," says Mike Scioscia, catcher for the Dodgers, "a pitch to

Dwight "Doc" Gooden won the Cy Young in his rookie year, 1985.
He led the league in ERA, wins and strikeouts.

a hitter is decided by the next two or three batters coming up."

Many other things can make or break a pitcher going for a Cy Young award. Does his home park favor home run hitters? Does he play on artificial turf? Does he get good fielding from the other players? Is he a good fielder himself? Does his team supply enough runs to help him win? Many pitchers who failed to win the award came up short for just these reasons.

Many things make up a Cy Young winner, including pitching, fielding, being in the right place at the right time, and knowing when to throw the right pitches. The fun is in watching to see who will be the next to make the list.

20 Strikeouts

Scene: April 29, 1986, Boston's Fenway Park.
Teams: The Boston Red Sox vs. the Seattle Mariners.
Background: The Boston Celtics of the NBA are in a playoff basketball game at Boston Gardens. There are only 13,414 fans at the ballpark. These fans will see something that has never been accomplished in the 111 years of professional baseball.
Action: Roger Clemens is approaching exhaustion. His legs are cramping. The pressure is tremendous. His Red Sox are ahead 3-1 over the Mariners with one inning to go. Clemens has already struck out 18 batters. He's only one strikeout short of the Major League record, an opportunity that might never come again.

"Rocket," his teammate Al Nipper says, "do you realize that you're one away from tying the strikeout record?" Clemens tries to ignore him and concentrate on the task at hand.

The first batter Clemens faces in the ninth inning is Mariner shortstop Spike Owen. With as much strength as he can muster, Clemens fires off his fastball.

Boston ace Roger Clemens became the highest paid player of the 1991 season, earning some $5 million per year.

A strike. Two more fastballs, and Owen is down. With 19 strikeouts, Clemens joins three other pitchers with the record. Two batters to go.

The players and fans are on their feet. Mariner leftfielder Phil Bradley approaches the batter's box. Even though Bradley knows he is facing one of the fastest pitchers in the game today, there's little he can do about it. Clemens winds up. Three fastballs blow past Bradley, and Clemens owns the record. The last batter up grounds out, but by then it doesn't matter. Roger Clemens is on top, the only man to ever strike out 20 batters in a nine-inning game.

Clemens continued to use his 93-97 mph fastball that year. In 1986 he won 24 games, led his team to the World Series, and won his first of two Cy Young Awards in a row.

But his mark of 20 strikeouts in a single game may stand a long time. "I've watched perfect games by Catfish Hunter and Mike Witt," said his manager John McNamara. "But this was the most awesome pitching performance I've ever seen."

Leroy Robert "Satchel" Paige was a great pitcher who wasn't allowed to play with white players until late in his career.

Coming Up Short

The Cy Young is awarded to a pitcher for putting together a remarkable season in any given year. Still, there are some great pitchers who have never won the award. Some of these pitchers have (and will) make it to Baseball's Hall of Fame.

Juan Marichal was a power pitcher with control. He had a fancy high kick when he delivered. Those two qualities made him inspiring to watch. In a four-year period he won 93 games. He had more than 200 strikeouts six different seasons. His ERA was always low. One big reason Marichal never won the Cy Young was Sandy Koufax. When Marichal had a great year, Koufax had a greater year.

Sports medicine today has prolonged many careers. For example, everyone thought Tommy John was finished because of injuries. But after elbow surgery, he was better than before. Though he never won the Cy Young, he won 288 games, number 21 on the all-time list.

Don Sutton continued winning after he turned 40 through conditioning. He relied on his legs more than his arm, and took good care of himself. His conditioning paid off. Sutton is 12th on the lifetime pitching list with 324 wins.

Phil Niekro was able to keep on going by specializing in a less-stressful pitch, the knuckleball. The knuckleball helped him to save his arm and win many of his 318 games after he turned 40.

The ageless Nolan Ryan has the record for career strikeouts (more than 5,300) and no-hitters (7), but no Cy Young award.

Bert Blyleven had one of the greatest curveballs ever. Although he gave up a lot of home runs, he also got a lot of wins. With his curve and control, Blyleven continues to approach the 300 victory mark.

When certain words are mentioned, people think of Nolan Ryan:

- Strikeouts—Ryan has more lifetime than anyone, including 383 in one season.
- Fastball—In his prime, Ryan was clocked at over 100 miles per hour.
- No-hitters—Ryan has pitched seven in his career, three more than his next closest competitor.
- Longevity—Ryan's most recent no-hitter came in 1991 when he was 44.

Alas, no one thinks of Ryan when the Cy Young Award is mentioned. Even though Ryan was one of the most overpowering and unhittable pitchers to ever throw the ball, he still doesn't have a Cy Young.

Until recently, some people thought Ryan wouldn't make it in the Hall of Fame. Control was a problem. Though he got a lot of strikeouts, he also lost a lot of games. But in 1990 Ryan finally hit the 300-win mark. He hopes to continue pitching as long as his fastball keeps working. Ryan is proof that some great pitchers don't always win all the awards.

Cy Young Day

Scene: Cy Young Day, August 13, 1908, the old Huntington Avenue grounds in Boston.

Teams: The Boston Red Sox vs. the American League All-Stars.

Background: Cy Young is in the twilight of his career. He's playing what would be his last year for the Boston Red Sox. A little over a month ago, Cy pitched a no-hitter. At age 41, he's the oldest player to accomplish such a feat (until Nolan Ryan breaks the record in 1990 at age 43). To honor a lifetime of greatness, the *Boston Post* is sponsoring this "Cy Young Day."

Action: It is Cy Young's "going out" party. Although he will pitch for three more seasons, 1908 is his last truly great year. The American League has postponed its games today—it's Cy's day. They have sent an all-star team to Boston to play the Red Sox in an exhibition game. It's the last chance for the league to say thanks to the greatest pitcher who ever played.

The fans come out in droves. Within an hour of opening, the park is filled. 10,000 people are turned away. The 20,000 who got seats will not be disappointed. They will witness what Cy described as his most memorable day. He pitches the first two innings of the exhibition game before leaving with arms full of flowers and a lifetime of memories.

Cy Young went on to win 21 games that year, losing 11. At season's end he was traded back to Cleveland where it all began. He won 19 games in 1909, seven in 1910, and three more in 1911 before finishing the season with the Boston Braves. He won four more for the Braves before hanging up his mitt for good.

Cy had always longed for his small town lifestyle in Eastern Ohio. After leaving baseball, he retired with his wife to the farm, always supporting the sport that gave him his living. In 1937, Cy was inducted into baseball's Hall of Fame.

In 1955, at the age of 88, Cy Young died from a heart attack. He was sitting in his favorite armchair, looking across the beautiful pasture lands, where he no doubt had thrown a ball or two.

Glossary

CHANGE-UP. Pitch thrown for a change of pace. Usually a slow pitch thrown after one or more fastballs. Also called a "slow ball."

CONTROL. Ability to throw strikes.

CURVEBALL. Pitch thrown with spin and snap of the wrist that causes it to curve when it reaches the plate.

EARNED RUN AVERAGE (ERA). A statistic that tells how many runs a pitcher gives up per nine innings. For instance, if a pitcher gave up three runs in three games, his ERA would be 1.00. A good ERA is usually anything under 3.00.

FASTBALL. Pitch thrown with power and speed. It is the most common pitch in baseball.

FORKBALL. See split-finger fastball.

GREASEBALL. An illegal pitch in which some substance has been added to the ball to give it strange movement. The substance can be anything from hair gel to petroleum jelly.

KNUCKLE BALL. A pitch thrown slowly with little or no spin. This causes it to react to the weather. The batter (and catcher and pitcher) never knows how it will approach. It is thrown by gripping with knuckles, finger tips or fingernails. Also called a "knuckler."

SCREWBALL. A pitch that curves in the direction of the throwing arm.

SHUTOUT. A game in which the losing team doesn't score.

SINKING BALL. A pitch that drops as it comes to the plate—"sinker."

SLIDER. A fastball with a curve on the end. It is thrown by sliding it out of the hand.

SPLIT-FINGER FASTBALL. The "pitch of the '80s." It looks like a fastball, has the speed of the changeup, and drops like a spitter.

STRIKE ZONE. Imaginary area that serves as target for pitcher to get a strike—from about the armpit of the batter to the top of his knee.

Bibliography

Aaseng, Nathan. *Steve Carlton—Baseball's Silent Strongman*. Minneapolis: Lerner Publications Company, 1984.

Belsky, Dick. *Tom Seaver—Baseball's Superstar*. New York: David McKay Company, Inc., 1977.

Campbell, Dave, Denny Matthews, Brooks Robinson, and Duke Snider. *The Scouting Report: 1985*. New York: Harper & Row, 1985.

Dickson, Paul. *The Dickson Baseball Dictionary*. New York: Facts on File, 1989.

Drucker, Malka. *Tom Seaver—Portrait of a Pitcher*. New York: Holiday House, 1978.

Einstein, Charles. *The Fireside Book of Baseball*. New York: Simon and Schuster, 1956.

Gutman, Bill. *More Modern Baseball Superstars*. New York: Dodd, Mead & Company, 1978.

Gutman, Bill. *New Breed of Heroes In Pro Baseball*. New York: Julian Messner, 1974.

Hano, Arnold. *Sandy Koufax Strikeout King*. New York & Toronto: Longmans Canada Limited. 1966.

Hollander, Zander. *The Complete Handbook of Baseball*. New York: New American Library, 1981.

Kickey, Glenn. *The Great No-Hitters*. Randnor: Chilton Book Company, 1976.

Libby, Bill. *Star Pitchers of the Major Leagues*. New York: Random House, 1971.

Luciano, Ron. *Baseball Lite*. New York: Bantam Books, 1990.

Puigley, Martin. *The Crooked Pitch*. Chapel Hill: Algonquin Books, 1984.

Reichler, Joseph. *Baseball's Great Moments*. New York: Crown Publishers, Inc., 1981.

Reidenbaugh, Lowell. *Cooperstown Where Baseball's Legends Live Forever*. St. Louis: The Sporting News Publishing Co., 1983.

Ritter, Lawrence, and Donald Honig. *The 100 Greatest Baseball Players of All Time*. New York: Crown Publishers, Inc., 1986.

Shapiro, Milton J. *Baseball's Greatest Pitchers*. New York: Simon & Schuster, Inc., 1969.

Smith, Robert. *Baseball*. New York: Simon and Schuster, 1970.

Thorn, John, and John B. Holway. *The Pitcher*. New York: Prentice Hall Press, 1987.

Index

About the Author

Marty Nabhan, a freelance writer, has published numerous articles and books for young people. His other books include *Mr. Magruder's Magical Mystical Bike Shop*, and *Australia*. In 1986, Marty covered the Transworld International Skateboard Championship in Vancouver, Canada, for the movie Radical Moves. An avid sports nut, he enjoys scuba diving, rock climbing, and backpacking. He is currently working on a movie about Yellowstone National Park. Marty and his lovely wife Wendy live in Southern California.

Photo Credits